Grok AI

Unlocking the Future of Artificial Intelligence, Deep Learning, and Neural Networks

TABLE OF CONTENTS

INTRODUCTION

Artificial Intelligence (AI) has become one of the most transformative technologies of the 21st century, influencing everything from healthcare and finance to entertainment and education. The rapid advancement of AI has made it an integral part of our daily lives, shaping how we interact with technology and how industries operate. Among the many innovations in AI, Grok AI stands out as a significant advancement that is pushing the boundaries of what AI can achieve. In this section, we will explore what Grok AI is, why it's generating so much buzz in the tech community, and why it's positioned to play a crucial role in the future of artificial intelligence. Whether you are a tech enthusiast, a developer, or someone simply curious about the advancements in AI, this book aims to break down Grok AI in a way that's both comprehensive and accessible.

> What is Grok AI?

At its core, Grok AI is an advanced AI system designed to leverage cutting-edge deep learning techniques to process and analyze complex datasets in ways that were once unimaginable. It represents a leap forward in the AI field, particularly in its ability to solve problems that require nuanced understanding and adaptability. Grok AI combines the power of neural networks, machine learning algorithms, and vast data processing capabilities to offer a system that not only understands data but also learns from it in real-time.

Grok AI isn't just another machine learning model; it's a system capable of self-improvement. This means it can analyze patterns in data, adapt to new information, and evolve its strategies over time without human intervention. This self-learning capability allows Grok AI to tackle a wide range of tasks, from natural language processing (NLP) and computer vision to predictive analytics and autonomous decision-making. The name "Grok" itself, derived from the science fiction novel Stranger in a Strange Land by Robert A. Heinlein, carries the connotation of understanding something profoundly and intuitively. This aligns perfectly with Grok AI's design: it aims to understand data, context, and scenarios in a way that mirrors human cognitive abilities. As a result, it offers enhanced accuracy and efficiency, making it an ideal solution for industries that require high levels of precision and automation.

> **Importance of AI in Today's World**

Artificial Intelligence is no longer a distant concept; it's a reality shaping industries and economies worldwide. AI systems are already present in many aspects of our lives, from the voice assistants on our smartphones to the recommendation engines on streaming platforms. The ability of AI to automate complex tasks, recognize patterns, and process vast amounts of data has transformed various sectors, including healthcare, manufacturing, retail, and more. AI's role in healthcare, for instance, cannot be overstated. From drug discovery to diagnosing diseases, AI systems like Grok AI are helping researchers and doctors process medical data faster and more accurately. In finance, AI is being used to predict stock market trends, detect fraud, and manage risk in ways that were previously impossible. AI's ability to analyze real-time data and make decisions quickly has also found applications in areas like autonomous vehicles and smart cities, making urban environments safer and more efficient.

What sets Grok AI apart from traditional AI systems is its level of adaptability and learning capabilities. While most AI systems require human intervention to reprogram or adjust their models when new data comes in, Grok AI is designed to learn autonomously. This makes it particularly effective in dynamic environments where the conditions are constantly changing. This adaptability is key to AI's increasing importance in industries where time-sensitive decisions must be made, and real-time data is abundant. The ability to improve itself without manual input means that Grok AI can scale efficiently, handling even the most complex tasks that were once thought to require human intelligence. This has vast implications not only for businesses looking to automate their operations but also for researchers, governments, and non-profits aiming to solve global challenges like climate change, poverty, and public health.

> Why Grok AI is Changing the Game

The AI landscape is crowded with various models and frameworks, but Grok AI represents a new frontier. It stands out because it pushes the boundaries of traditional machine learning and neural networks, integrating them in a way that enhances both performance and flexibility. One of the key aspects of Grok AI that sets it apart is its focus on both supervised and unsupervised learning. Unlike other AI systems that excel in one area but struggle in another, Grok AI can effectively balance these learning modes, adapting to a wide variety of data types and problem sets. The self-learning and evolving capabilities of Grok AI also mean it is more efficient in processing and analyzing data over time. As it continues to receive new information, it doesn't simply add that data to its existing knowledge base; it also reevaluates its methods and adjusts accordingly. This allows Grok AI to improve its accuracy and performance without requiring constant oversight, reducing the need for human intervention.

Another game-changing aspect of Grok AI is its ability to handle unstructured data. In the past, AI systems often struggled to process raw data that didn't fit neatly into predefined categories. However, Grok AI excels in this area, making it particularly useful in industries where data comes in a variety of forms, such as text, images, and video. This versatility opens up new possibilities in fields like natural language processing, computer vision, and speech recognition, where unstructured data is the norm. Moreover, Grok AI offers the flexibility to be applied across a wide range of industries. From healthcare and finance to marketing and logistics, Grok AI has the potential to revolutionize business operations by automating complex tasks and providing insights that would otherwise take humans hours, if not days, to uncover.

> Purpose and Scope of This Book

The purpose of this book is to provide a comprehensive and clear understanding of Grok AI, its capabilities, and its impact on the world of artificial intelligence. Whether you're a developer interested in the technical underpinnings of Grok AI or a business leader looking to understand how to integrate this technology into your organization, this book aims to provide valuable insights at every level.

Throughout the chapters, we will explore the core concepts behind Grok AI, including its architecture, training processes, and real-world applications. We will also delve into its key features, including its ability to self-learn, process complex datasets, and adapt to changing environments. Moreover, we will examine the broader implications of Grok AI's advancements, including ethical considerations, the future of work, and the potential for AI to solve global challenges. Each chapter is designed to build upon the previous one, gradually increasing in depth and complexity as we move from understanding the basic principles of AI to exploring the specific technologies behind Grok AI. By the end of this book, you will have a solid understanding of how Grok AI works, why it's such a powerful tool, and how it is shaping the future of AI technology.

Whether you're looking to implement Grok AI in your business, engage with its development as a researcher, or simply understand its potential, this book will serve as your guide to one of the most exciting and impactful AI systems to date.

In the following chapters, we will explore the technical aspects of Grok AI in detail, examining how it is changing the way AI systems learn, adapt, and process data. You'll also learn about the real-world applications of Grok AI and how it's already making an impact across a wide range of industries. Whether you're a seasoned AI professional or a newcomer to the field, the insights provided here will help you better understand the capabilities and potential of Grok AI.

CHAPTER 1

The Evolution of Artificial Intelligence

1.1 The Early Days of AI

Artificial Intelligence (AI), in its modern form, traces its roots back to the mid-20th century. The term itself was coined in 1956 by John McCarthy, who defined AI as "the science and engineering of making intelligent machines." The concept was grounded in the idea that machines could perform tasks that, when done by humans, require intelligence. At the heart of early AI was the work of British mathematician and logician Alan Turing. Turing's famous test, now known as the Turing Test, was proposed in 1950 to determine if a machine could exhibit intelligent behavior indistinguishable from that of a human. The test essentially asks whether a machine can engage in a conversation that is indistinguishable from a conversation between two humans. Although the Turing Test itself has seen debate, it laid the philosophical groundwork for how machines might mimic human cognition.

The 1950s and 1960s saw optimism in AI research. Early systems, known as rule-based systems or expert systems, followed predefined logic to solve problems. These systems operated on simple decision trees and if-then statements, offering solutions in narrowly defined problem spaces. However, these systems lacked the ability to handle uncertainty or learn from experience. This limitation became clear, and research faced setbacks.

The AI Winter refers to a period in the 1970s and 1980s when expectations of AI far outpaced its actual capabilities. AI funding and research dwindled, primarily due to the inability of early systems to solve real-world problems or meet the ambitious promises of researchers. However, in the late 1980s and early 1990s, AI experienced a revival, largely fueled by advancements in machine learning (ML), a subfield of AI that focused on algorithms capable of improving through experience. This period marked a shift from simple rule-based systems to more dynamic and adaptive models.

1.2 Key Milestones in AI Development

> From Rule-based Systems to Machine Learning

AI's early rule-based systems were limited by their static nature. A shift occurred with the introduction of machine learning (ML), a subfield of AI where computers learn from data rather than being explicitly programmed. Early machine learning systems applied simple statistical models to data, enabling them to improve performance with more data. This was a significant leap forward as it allowed systems to adapt and improve without human intervention. During the late 1990s and early 2000s, machine learning began to gain real-world applications. The most notable example was IBM's Deep Blue, which defeated the world chess champion, Garry Kasparov, in 1997. This was a demonstration of a powerful machine learning algorithm capable of evaluating millions of possible moves in a game of chess.

However, even with these advances, traditional machine learning models were limited in their ability to process complex data. The breakthrough came with the rise of deep learning, which would radically transform AI.

> Breakthroughs in Natural Language Processing (NLP)

Parallel to developments in machine learning, significant progress was made in Natural Language Processing (NLP), a branch of AI focused on making sense of human language. Early attempts in NLP involved parsing sentences and recognizing patterns in text through rule-based methods. These systems could translate words or process speech, but they lacked understanding or the ability to generate meaningful responses.

The turning point came with statistical methods and, later, deep learning techniques applied to language. In 2013, researchers introduced word embeddings, mathematical representations of words that capture semantic meaning. This approach allowed machines to understand context and relationships between words, which was a breakthrough in how machines understood human language.

Recent advancements in NLP, powered by transformer models such as OpenAI's GPT-3 and Google's BERT, have enabled machines to generate coherent and contextually relevant text, understand sentiment, and even hold conversations. These models use vast amounts of text data to learn the patterns of human language, dramatically improving AI's capabilities in customer service, content creation, and translation.

1.3 Understanding Deep Learning and Neural Networks

> What Makes Deep Learning Different?

Deep learning is a subset of machine learning that focuses on models inspired by the neural architecture of the human brain, specifically designed to work with large amounts of data. Traditional machine learning algorithms require manual feature extraction, where humans define the characteristics of the data to focus on. However, deep learning models, particularly deep neural networks, can automatically learn hierarchical features from raw data, making them far more powerful in tasks like image recognition, speech processing, and even game playing. Deep learning models are structured as layers of artificial neurons that process information. The first layer identifies basic features such as edges in an image, while deeper layers combine these features to recognize more complex patterns like faces or objects. This ability to extract complex representations from simple ones is one of deep learning's most significant advantages over traditional machine learning approaches.

The most significant development in deep learning has been the Convolutional Neural Network (CNN), primarily used in image recognition and computer vision. CNNs have drastically improved object detection, facial recognition, and even medical image analysis. Other architectures like Recurrent Neural Networks (RNNs) and Long Short-Term Memory (LSTM) networks have been pivotal in speech recognition and language modeling, enabling machines to process sequential data such as text or speech.

> Neural Networks: The Brain Behind AI

At the core of deep learning is the neural network, a computational model designed to simulate the way the human brain processes information. A neural network consists of layers of nodes, or neurons, that are connected to each other. Each connection between neurons has a weight, which is adjusted during the learning process. The learning process in a neural network involves adjusting these weights through backpropagation, where the model iteratively improves its predictions by minimizing errors. When given an input, the model makes a prediction, compares it to the actual result, and adjusts its weights accordingly to reduce the error. This process continues until the model achieves the desired accuracy. As neural networks are fed more data, they continuously adjust and improve, making them highly adaptable and capable of handling complex tasks.

Neural networks are responsible for powering many of the AI applications we use today, from autonomous vehicles to recommendation systems and real-time language translation. Their ability to learn directly from data, without needing explicit programming for every task, is what makes them so powerful.

1.4 Grok AI's Place in AI Evolution

> Grok's Foundational Concepts

Grok AI represents the next step in the evolution of AI. Built on the foundations of machine learning, deep learning, and neural networks, Grok AI offers a more integrated and advanced approach to solving complex problems. It is designed to process a vast array of data, including structured and unstructured formats, and deliver insights that were once out of reach for traditional AI models. One of Grok AI's foundational principles is contextual understanding. While traditional AI systems are good at processing data and making predictions based on patterns, Grok AI takes this a step further by incorporating contextual awareness. This means Grok AI can not only process data but also understand its nuances and relationships to real-world contexts, making it especially powerful in dynamic, unpredictable environments.

Another key concept in Grok AI is its ability to evolve. Traditional AI models often require retraining with new data to adapt to changes, but Grok AI can learn continuously, adjusting its models based on real-time data and experiences without manual intervention. This continuous learning makes it highly adaptable and suitable for applications in fields such as finance, healthcare, and autonomous driving, where data and environments change constantly.

> **How Grok AI Advances Traditional Models**

Grok AI advances traditional models by introducing multi-modal learning, enabling it to process various types of data (text, images, audio, etc.) simultaneously. This allows Grok AI to make more comprehensive decisions by understanding complex, multi-faceted input. It integrates the best aspects of deep learning, reinforcement learning, and unsupervised learning into a single system, allowing it to perform tasks like real-time decision-making, predictive analytics, and personalized recommendations more efficiently.

Grok AI also excels in scalability. While traditional AI models struggle to maintain performance as data sets grow larger, Grok AI's architecture allows it to scale without sacrificing accuracy or speed. This makes it an ideal solution for enterprises that require the processing of massive datasets, such as social media platforms or global supply chains.

Lastly, Grok AI's use of explainability sets it apart from other AI models. One of the criticisms of deep learning models is their "black-box" nature, where it is difficult to understand how a model arrived at a particular decision. Grok AI integrates explainable AI (XAI) principles, allowing users to gain insight into how the system made its decisions, making it a more transparent and trustworthy solution. In this way, Grok AI pushes the boundaries of traditional models, integrating new techniques and methodologies to provide more accurate, adaptable, and explainable AI solutions. As AI continues to evolve, Grok AI represents the cutting edge of this technological revolution, positioning itself as a key player in shaping the future of AI.

CHAPTER 2

Deep Dive into Grok AI

> What is Grok AI?

Grok AI is an advanced artificial intelligence system designed to tackle the challenges posed by complex, real-world problems. Unlike traditional AI models, which often rely on predefined rule sets or static data, Grok AI is built to learn from experience and adapt to new situations autonomously. This system is an embodiment of deep learning and neural network methodologies, leveraging large datasets to continuously improve and make more accurate predictions. At its core, Grok AI has a flexible architecture that integrates multiple technologies to process and interpret information. It mimics the cognitive processes of the human brain, learning from vast amounts of input data and using that knowledge to make decisions or recommendations. The AI's architecture is designed to scale effortlessly, allowing it to function across various sectors, from healthcare to finance, and even creative industries like content generation.

> Overview of Grok AI's Architecture

Grok AI is built on an architecture that includes multiple layers of neural networks, designed to process data in a hierarchical manner. This architecture ensures that the system can learn from different levels of abstraction, starting with basic information and gradually building up to more complex representations. This is a core characteristic of deep learning, where each layer of the network extracts progressively more meaningful features from the raw data. The system is composed of several modules that work together to enhance performance and adaptability. At the lowest layer, raw data such as images, text, or numerical inputs are processed and transformed into a more usable format. These transformations occur in successive layers, with each layer's output serving as the input for the next. This stacked approach allows Grok AI to identify increasingly abstract features and patterns within the data.

> **Comparison with Traditional AI Models**

Traditional AI models rely heavily on rule-based systems, where developers manually define the logic that governs the AI's decision-making. These models can perform specific tasks very efficiently but lack the ability to learn from new data without human intervention. In contrast, Grok AI is based on neural networks and machine learning algorithms that enable it to autonomously improve over time as it is exposed to more data.

One major difference between Grok AI and traditional AI is that Grok AI does not require explicit programming for every task it performs. Instead, it uses large datasets to train the model, allowing it to identify patterns and make predictions on its own. This learning capability means that Grok AI can handle more complex, unstructured data, like images or natural language, more efficiently than traditional systems.

2.2 Core Technologies Driving Grok AI

Grok AI stands out because of its combination of deep learning, machine learning algorithms, and neural network principles, which form the backbone of its operation. These technologies allow Grok AI to process large volumes of data, recognize patterns, and improve its performance in real-time. Below, we explore how these core technologies work together to give Grok AI its advanced capabilities.

> Machine Learning Algorithms in Grok

Machine learning is central to Grok AI's functionality. It enables the system to learn from data without being explicitly programmed for each specific task. Grok AI uses supervised, unsupervised, and reinforcement learning techniques to process data and improve its performance. Supervised learning involves training the AI on labeled datasets, where the correct output is known. The model learns the relationship between inputs and outputs, making it suitable for tasks like classification and regression. Unsupervised learning allows Grok AI to find patterns and structures in data without predefined labels.

This type of learning is particularly useful in scenarios where the AI needs to discover hidden relationships within large sets of unstructured data, such as clustering similar items or identifying anomalies. Reinforcement learning involves teaching the AI through trial and error. It learns by receiving feedback from its environment based on the actions it takes, helping Grok AI optimize its decision-making process in dynamic, unpredictable situations, such as real-time strategy or robotics. By combining these different methods, Grok AI can continuously adapt to new information and become more accurate in its predictions and decision-making.

> **The Role of Neural Networks**

Neural networks are the driving force behind Grok AI's ability to process complex, high-dimensional data. These networks are inspired by the structure of the human brain and consist of interconnected layers of nodes, each representing a unit of computation. Each node receives input from the previous layer, processes it, and passes its output to the next layer. Neural networks come in various types, such as feedforward networks, convolutional neural networks (CNNs), and recurrent neural networks (RNNs). Each of these network types excels in different areas:

- Feedforward Neural Networks are used for simple classification tasks, where the input flows in one direction through the layers.

- Convolutional Neural Networks (CNNs) are optimized for image processing, making them ideal for tasks like object detection and image recognition.

- Recurrent Neural Networks (RNNs) are used for sequential data, such as time-series analysis and natural language processing (NLP), where the output of one step influences the next.

In Grok AI, neural networks are trained on vast datasets and continuously updated, allowing the system to make more informed and accurate decisions over time.

2.3 Key Features of Grok AI

Grok AI is not just an advanced system in terms of its underlying technologies but also in its practical features that enhance its usability and effectiveness. These features enable Grok AI to be versatile and adaptable across various domains.

> Learning Capabilities and Adaptation

One of Grok AI's key features is its ability to learn from experience. Unlike traditional AI systems that operate on static data, Grok AI evolves as it interacts with new data, improving its performance continuously. The system uses feedback loops to refine its models, making it capable of adapting to changes in the environment or data patterns without needing human intervention. For instance, in a business context, Grok AI could analyze sales data, learn from past trends, and adjust marketing strategies based on new consumer behaviors. This capacity for self-improvement makes Grok AI highly effective in dynamic industries where data is constantly changing.

> **Autonomous Decision-Making**

Grok AI's autonomous decision-making ability is another standout feature. The system doesn't require constant human oversight to function effectively. Instead, it can analyze the situation, weigh the options, and make decisions independently, optimizing for specific goals. This autonomous decision-making ability is particularly useful in industries like finance, where AI systems must react to real-time market data, or in healthcare, where Grok AI can analyze medical images and make diagnostic recommendations based on its learned knowledge.

By leveraging both deep learning and reinforcement learning, Grok AI can continually refine its decision-making process, ensuring that its actions are always based on the most up-to-date and accurate data.

2.4 Grok AI's Unique Approach to AI Challenges

One of the reasons Grok AI stands out from traditional AI models is its innovative approach to solving complex challenges. The system excels in handling large datasets, particularly when that data is noisy, unstructured, or lacks clear patterns.

> How It Handles Complex Data

Data complexity is a major challenge in AI development. Grok AI has been specifically designed to tackle this issue by utilizing its deep learning models to process diverse and voluminous datasets. Whether it is image data, sensor data, or text-based information, Grok AI can parse and extract meaningful insights, regardless of the data's inherent complexity. For example, in healthcare, Grok AI can process medical images that are noisy or incomplete, extracting useful information despite the imperfections. In natural language processing, Grok AI can understand and respond to unstructured text, like social media posts, to identify sentiments and trends.

> Scalability and Flexibility

Another significant strength of Grok AI is its scalability and flexibility. As industries generate more and more data, AI systems must be able to scale to handle increased processing demands. Grok AI's architecture allows it to scale up efficiently, ensuring it can handle larger datasets and more complex tasks as it grows. Furthermore, Grok AI's flexibility means it can be adapted to various domains. Whether it's healthcare, finance, marketing, or robotics, Grok AI can be tailored to meet the unique needs of any industry. This versatility is crucial in a rapidly evolving technological landscape, where AI applications are constantly expanding.

Grok AI represents the next step in AI evolution, combining cutting-edge technologies like deep learning, machine learning algorithms, and neural networks to create a powerful, adaptive, and autonomous system. Its ability to learn from vast datasets and improve over time, coupled with its flexibility and scalability, makes Grok AI a leader in the AI field.

CHAPTER 3

Deep Learning and Neural Networks in AI

3.1 What is Deep Learning?

Deep learning is a subfield of machine learning that seeks to replicate the way humans learn from experience. It involves training algorithms to recognize patterns, make predictions, and automate decision-making processes. Unlike traditional machine learning, which requires explicit programming for specific tasks, deep learning allows the model to learn directly from vast amounts of data, making it incredibly powerful for complex tasks like image recognition, speech processing, and natural language understanding. At the core of deep learning lies the neural network. A neural network is a structure inspired by the human brain, consisting of interconnected layers of nodes, each designed to simulate the activity of neurons in the brain. Deep learning models consist of multiple layers, hence the term "deep." The depth of these layers allows the system to build highly abstract representations of data, making it particularly suited for applications that require understanding intricate patterns.

> How Deep Learning Models Work

Deep learning models operate by transforming data through layers of interconnected neurons. When data enters a deep learning model, it is passed through the input layer and propagated through subsequent hidden layers, where it undergoes transformations. These transformations occur through the application of weights, which are adjusted during the training process to minimize errors and optimize performance.

The key to deep learning's power is its ability to automatically learn hierarchical features from raw data. In simple terms, as the data passes through the layers, the model learns to recognize basic features in the lower layers (like edges or corners in an image) and progressively combines them into more complex representations in the deeper layers (like objects or faces). This hierarchical learning enables deep learning models to handle unstructured data like images, sound, and text in a way that traditional models cannot.

> Layers, Nodes, and Activation Functions

A deep learning model typically consists of three types of layers: the input layer, hidden layers, and the output layer. The input layer receives the raw data, while the hidden layers process the information, and the output layer provides the final prediction or classification. Nodes, or "neurons," are the fundamental units in these layers. Each node performs a mathematical operation on the data it receives and passes the result to the next layer. These operations are controlled by weights and biases, which adjust during the training process to minimize the error in the network's predictions.

The role of activation functions is essential in neural networks. These functions decide whether a neuron should be activated based on the weighted sum of inputs it receives. Without activation functions, neural networks would be limited to performing linear transformations, meaning they wouldn't be able to solve more complex, non-linear problems. Common activation functions include the sigmoid, tanh, and ReLU functions. ReLU (Rectified Linear Unit) is particularly popular in deep learning due to its simplicity and efficiency in handling the vanishing gradient problem, which occurs when gradients become too small to effectively update weights in deep networks.

3.2 Neural Networks: The Backbone of Deep Learning

Neural networks form the foundation of deep learning, and their structure mimics the connections between neurons in the human brain. The process of training a neural network involves adjusting the weights of these connections based on the error produced by the model's predictions compared to the actual values. This is done using algorithms like backpropagation, which helps propagate errors backward through the network, adjusting weights to minimize the loss.

> Anatomy of Neural Networks

The architecture of a neural network is typically composed of layers of neurons, including:

- Input Layer: The first layer where the raw data enters the network.

- Hidden Layers: These layers perform computations and transformations, discovering features in the data at multiple levels of abstraction. A network may have one or more hidden layers.

- Output Layer: The final layer that provides the model's prediction, which can be a classification label, a regression value, or another type of output.

Each of these layers contains neurons that are connected to each other, with each connection having an associated weight.

During training, the weights are updated using optimization techniques to reduce the prediction error.

> Types of Neural Networks Used in Grok AI

Grok AI utilizes various types of neural networks, each suited for different tasks. Some of the most commonly used neural network architectures in Grok AI include:

- Feedforward Neural Networks (FNNs): The most basic type of neural network, where information moves in one direction from the input to the output. These are ideal for classification tasks with structured data.

- Convolutional Neural Networks (CNNs): CNNs are specialized for tasks that involve grid-like data, such as images. They use convolutional layers that apply filters to the data, enabling the network to automatically learn spatial hierarchies and features. CNNs are heavily used in image recognition tasks in Grok AI.

- Recurrent Neural Networks (RNNs): RNNs are designed for sequential data, such as time series, speech, or text. They have loops that allow information to persist, making them ideal for tasks like language modeling or speech recognition. Long Short-Term Memory (LSTM) networks, a type of RNN, are often used to handle long-term dependencies in sequences.

- Generative Adversarial Networks (GANs): GANs consist of two neural networks, a generator and a discriminator, that compete against each other. They are often used for generating realistic images, videos, or text. In Grok AI, GANs can be used for data augmentation or content creation.

These networks, with their specialized layers and configurations, enable Grok AI to tackle a wide range of tasks with impressive efficiency.

3.3 The Training Process: From Data to Knowledge

Training a deep learning model involves feeding it data, allowing it to make predictions, and adjusting the model's parameters based on the error. This process is typically carried out through supervised learning, unsupervised learning, or reinforcement learning, depending on the task and the nature of the data.

> How Grok AI Learns Through Training

Grok AI's learning process involves presenting it with large amounts of labeled data, where the correct answers are known. During training, Grok AI adjusts the weights in its neural network to minimize the error between its predictions and the correct outcomes. The process of adjusting these weights is known as "training" and is usually done using an optimization algorithm like gradient descent.

- Gradient Descent: This algorithm helps minimize the error by updating the weights in the direction that reduces the cost function. Grok AI uses advanced variants like stochastic gradient descent (SGD) and Adam optimizer, which help the model converge faster and more efficiently.

- Backpropagation: Once the model makes a prediction, backpropagation is used to calculate the gradient of the error with respect to each weight in the network. These gradients are then used to update the weights.

Through this iterative process, Grok AI gradually improves its predictions, learning complex patterns in the data. This learning process is highly data-dependent, which is why Grok AI excels in tasks where vast amounts of labeled data are available.

> **Supervised vs. Unsupervised Learning**

Supervised Learning: In supervised learning, Grok AI is trained on labeled data, meaning each input comes with the correct output. The model learns to map inputs to the correct outputs. This method is ideal for tasks like image classification, speech recognition, and predictive modeling.

- Unsupervised Learning: In unsupervised learning, Grok AI is given data without explicit labels. Instead of predicting outcomes, the model tries to find patterns and structures in the data, such as grouping similar data points together (clustering) or reducing the dimensionality of the data. Unsupervised learning is often used in exploratory data analysis and anomaly detection.

- Semi-supervised Learning: Grok AI also employs semi-supervised learning, which is a mix of both supervised and unsupervised methods. This approach is particularly useful when only a small portion of the data is labeled.

3.4 Real-World Applications of Deep Learning

Deep learning, with its ability to learn from massive amounts of data and recognize intricate patterns, is transforming industries across the globe. Grok AI leverages deep learning models to solve complex problems in healthcare, finance, autonomous driving, and many other fields.

Healthcare, Finance, and Autonomous Vehicles

> Healthcare: Grok AI's deep learning capabilities are revolutionizing healthcare by automating diagnostics and improving personalized medicine. Through the use of CNNs, Grok AI can analyze medical images like X-rays and MRIs to detect diseases such as cancer, improving diagnostic accuracy and speed. Furthermore, Grok AI is employed in genomics to analyze DNA sequences and predict disease susceptibility.

> Finance: In the financial industry, deep learning models are used for fraud detection, algorithmic trading, and risk assessment. Grok AI's models can analyze historical financial data, identify patterns, and make predictions about future market movements, helping traders and investors make informed decisions.

> Autonomous Vehicles: Grok AI is at the forefront of developing self-driving car technology. By using deep learning models like CNNs for computer vision and RNNs for decision-making, Grok AI enables vehicles to recognize objects, make real-time driving decisions, and navigate complex environments. These advancements promise to reshape the future of transportation.

How Grok AI is Revolutionizing These Fields

Grok AI's application of deep learning models extends beyond traditional boundaries, bringing transformative solutions to industries. By automating tasks that were once thought to be solely within human capability, Grok AI is enhancing productivity, safety, and efficiency. Whether it's helping doctors diagnose faster, allowing businesses to predict market trends, or enabling vehicles to drive autonomously, Grok AI's deep learning models are unlocking new possibilities that were once unimaginable.

In each of these applications, Grok AI's ability to process large datasets, learn from them, and make decisions in real-time is setting it apart from other AI technologies, positioning it as a leader in the field. The future of AI, especially in deep learning, holds vast potential, and Grok AI is poised to continue leading the way in innovation and impact across industries.

CHAPTER 4

Grok AI's Data Processing Power

4.1 Data Collection and Preprocessing

> How Grok AI Gathers and Processes Data

In the context of Grok AI, data collection is the foundational step in the entire process of building intelligent systems. For AI to learn and make accurate predictions or decisions, it needs high-quality data from which to draw insights. Grok AI, leveraging advanced algorithms and techniques, processes large volumes of data from a wide variety of sources. These sources can include structured datasets, such as tables of numerical values, and unstructured data, like text, images, and audio files. The data collection process often begins with identifying reliable data sources. Grok AI can gather data from databases, APIs, user-generated inputs, IoT devices, and even real-time streams from social media platforms or sensors in the field. The diversity of these sources allows Grok AI to handle both static datasets and dynamic, real-time data, enhancing its capability to respond to new inputs without retraining from scratch.

Once the data is gathered, it undergoes a series of preprocessing steps to ensure it is clean and consistent. This preprocessing includes removing any noisy or irrelevant data points, handling missing values, and normalizing data so that the model can process it more efficiently. For instance, numerical data may need to be scaled, and categorical data might need to be encoded into a numerical format. This ensures that the input fed into Grok AI's machine learning models is ready for further analysis. Handling big data comes with its own set of challenges. Grok AI uses distributed systems and cloud-based infrastructure to manage vast amounts of information. This setup allows Grok AI to process data at scale, quickly extracting patterns and insights from large datasets without running into issues of storage or computational limits. Technologies like parallel processing and data sharding help Grok AI to divide large tasks into manageable chunks, ensuring that each segment of the data is processed efficiently.

> Handling Big Data and Complexity

Big data is defined not only by its sheer volume but also by its complexity. For AI systems like Grok to handle big data, they need to be equipped with mechanisms that can process various types of information simultaneously and effectively. Grok AI's ability to handle complex data comes from its robust preprocessing pipeline, which involves cleaning and transforming the data into a consistent, usable form. For instance, in scenarios where the data includes time-series information or geospatial data, Grok AI applies specialized techniques to ensure that these complex data formats are handled correctly. Time-series data, for example, might require time-based transformations, while geospatial data needs spatial encoding to allow AI models to process the underlying patterns in location-based information. Grok AI's ability to handle such intricate data types ensures that it can work effectively with diverse industries, such as healthcare, finance, or transportation, where big data and complex datasets are common.

4.2 Feature Engineering and Data Transformation

> Preparing Data for Neural Networks

Feature engineering is the process of selecting, modifying, or creating new features from raw data to improve the performance of machine learning models. Grok AI's data pipeline is optimized for feature engineering to ensure that the machine learning models it employs have the best possible input. In neural networks, data is passed through layers of artificial neurons, where each layer extracts features at different levels of abstraction. Grok AI prepares the data for this process by transforming it into a format that the neural network can effectively use. One of the critical steps in this process is feature scaling, which ensures that each feature has a similar range of values. This helps the model learn without being biased toward features with larger numerical ranges. Another essential aspect of feature engineering in Grok AI is feature extraction. For instance, when dealing with text data, Grok AI might use methods like word embeddings to convert words into vector representations that capture semantic meaning. Similarly, in image recognition tasks, Grok AI can employ techniques like convolutional neural networks (CNNs) to automatically extract features like edges and textures from raw image pixels.

By carefully selecting relevant features, Grok AI ensures that it only uses the most important aspects of the data for training its models. This process not only improves the efficiency of the AI but also ensures higher accuracy in its predictions and decisions.

> Selecting Relevant Features

The relevance of features is crucial for the model's predictive power. Including irrelevant or redundant features can decrease the model's performance and increase the time required for training. Grok AI addresses this issue by using automated techniques like Recursive

Feature Elimination (RFE) or mutual information scoring, which helps identify and retain only the most impactful features. Feature selection plays an essential role in making the model both efficient and interpretable. For example, in predictive maintenance systems used by manufacturers, selecting features related to machinery sensor data can help Grok AI predict potential failures. Irrelevant data, like external environmental factors that do not correlate with machine health, would be excluded. This targeted feature selection ensures that Grok AI's models are optimized for both speed and accuracy, using only the most important data inputs.

4.3 Managing and Using Structured and Unstructured Data

> Grok AI's Versatility in Data Types

Structured data consists of information that is neatly organized, often in tables with rows and columns, such as spreadsheets or databases. This type of data is easier for AI systems to process because it follows a consistent schema. On the other hand, unstructured data includes information that does not have a predefined structure, such as text, images, audio, and video. Grok AI is particularly versatile in handling both structured and unstructured data types. For structured data, it uses traditional machine learning algorithms like decision trees, linear regression, and support vector machines (SVMs). These models are designed to work well with tabular data and provide accurate predictions based on the relationships between input variables. For unstructured data, Grok AI leverages deep learning techniques, which are particularly effective for processing high-dimensional data like images, videos, and text. Convolutional Neural Networks (CNNs) are used for image and video recognition tasks, while Recurrent Neural Networks (RNNs) and Long Short-Term Memory (LSTM) networks excel in processing sequential data, such as natural language.

Grok AI's ability to seamlessly integrate structured and unstructured data allows it to work across multiple industries where these types of data are abundant. For example, in healthcare, Grok AI can analyze both structured data (such as patient records) and unstructured data (like medical images) to provide more comprehensive insights.

> Best Practices for Effective Data Use

To ensure that data is used effectively, Grok AI follows several best practices. One key aspect is maintaining data quality. This involves regular checks to ensure that the data is accurate, up-to-date, and free from errors. For example, when dealing with sensor data from industrial machines, it is essential to verify that the data is correctly recorded and not affected by hardware malfunctions. Another practice is ensuring that data is appropriately labeled and annotated. For supervised learning tasks, accurate labeling is crucial for model training. In the case of image recognition, for instance, each image in the dataset must be correctly labeled with the object or feature it represents. Grok AI often uses a combination of automated processes and manual labeling to ensure that data is correctly annotated.

Finally, Grok AI uses data augmentation techniques to artificially increase the size and diversity of training datasets. This is particularly useful when dealing with image or text data, as it allows Grok AI to simulate different variations of the data and increase model robustness. For example, in image classification, Grok AI might rotate or flip images to expose the model to different perspectives, improving its ability to generalize.

4.4 The Role of Data in Grok AI's Success

> How Grok AI Harnesses Data for Decision Making

Data is the foundation of Grok AI's ability to make intelligent decisions. Through a process known as training, Grok AI learns patterns and correlations within the data, which it then uses to make predictions or decisions. This ability to extract insights from vast amounts of data allows Grok AI to function in various applications, from predicting stock market trends to providing personalized recommendations in e-commerce. For example, in predictive analytics, Grok AI can analyze historical data to forecast future events. This could be used in fields like finance, where Grok AI might predict stock price movements based on historical trading data. Similarly, in marketing, Grok AI uses customer behavior data to predict which products a customer is most likely to purchase, thus enabling more targeted advertising.

> Data Security and Ethics in AI

As AI systems like Grok become more powerful, ensuring the security of the data they process is critical. Grok AI uses state-of-the-art encryption methods to protect data both at rest and in transit. This prevents unauthorized access and ensures that sensitive information remains confidential. Equally important are the ethical implications of using data in AI systems. Grok AI follows strict guidelines to ensure that the data it uses is ethically sourced, and that the models it creates do not perpetuate harmful biases. This is especially crucial in sensitive areas like hiring or law enforcement, where biased AI models could have severe societal consequences. To maintain ethical standards, Grok AI incorporates transparency in its decision-making processes. This allows users to understand how the AI arrived at a particular decision, helping to build trust in the system. Grok AI also ensures that its data collection practices comply with regulations like the General Data Protection Regulation (GDPR), which mandates strict control over personal data. By combining robust data security measures with ethical data usage, Grok AI ensures that its data processing capabilities are not only powerful but also responsible and aligned with societal values.

CHAPTER 5

Grok AI in Natural Language Processing (NLP)

5.1 Understanding NLP and Its Importance

Natural Language Processing (NLP) is a critical subfield of artificial intelligence (AI) that focuses on the interaction between computers and human languages. Its purpose is to allow machines to understand, interpret, and generate human language in a way that is both meaningful and useful. NLP is fundamental to how AI can engage with people, making communication more efficient between humans and machines.

> NLP Fundamentals: Speech, Text, and Understanding

At its core, NLP is concerned with the complexities of language, which is often filled with nuances, ambiguities, and varying structures. The fundamental goal of NLP is to enable computers to process and make sense of human language in all its forms—spoken, written, or even signed. For computers to truly understand language, they must first break down the components of speech and text into manageable units that the machine can work with.

In spoken language, NLP systems must deal with phonemes, syllables, and sentences while interpreting context, tone, and intent. In written language, NLP systems examine sentence structure, word meanings, and context within a paragraph or larger text. The ability of a machine to process both types of input allows for a broader set of applications and enables AI to engage in conversations, translate languages, or even summarize content. A key concept in NLP is parsing, which is the process of breaking down a sentence into its components to understand grammatical structure and meaning. This allows an AI system to identify parts of speech (such as nouns, verbs, and adjectives), relationships between words, and overall sentence sentiment.

> Applications in Everyday Life

NLP has already permeated many aspects of daily life. Voice assistants like Apple's Siri, Amazon's Alexa, and Google Assistant all rely on NLP to process and respond to user requests. These systems use NLP algorithms to convert spoken language into text, analyze the intent behind the speech, and produce an appropriate response. Similarly, email filtering systems use NLP to categorize messages and flag those that may contain spam or contain certain keywords. In social media, NLP is used for sentiment analysis, enabling brands to track public opinion by analyzing how people talk about their products. Moreover, NLP is widely used in translation software, such as Google Translate, which enables users to convert text or speech from one language to another. These systems rely on sophisticated NLP models that account for the grammatical and syntactic differences between languages, making it possible to provide more accurate translations.

5.2 How Grok AI Understands and Processes Language

Grok AI, with its advanced capabilities, takes NLP to the next level by implementing deep learning models that allow the system to process language in a more sophisticated manner. Unlike traditional NLP methods that rely heavily on predefined rules and dictionaries, Grok AI leverages modern machine learning techniques to understand language dynamically, learning patterns from vast amounts of data.

> Deep Learning Models for NLP

Deep learning models, particularly those based on neural networks, are key to Grok AI's NLP capabilities. These models consist of multiple layers of artificial neurons that simulate the human brain's way of processing information. For NLP tasks, deep learning models, such as transformers, have become increasingly popular. Transformers, introduced in the 2017 paper "Attention is All You Need," revolutionized NLP by using an attention mechanism that allows models to weigh the importance of different words in a sentence relative to each other, even if they are far apart. Grok AI uses these models to handle a variety of NLP tasks, such as text classification, named entity recognition, and language generation. The deep learning framework enables the system to learn complex patterns in data without requiring explicit programming or feature engineering. Instead, Grok AI can learn directly from large corpora of text, extracting meaning and understanding relationships within the data.

> Grok AI's Language Processing Capabilities

What sets Grok AI apart from traditional NLP systems is its ability to handle more sophisticated language tasks with high accuracy. Grok AI can understand context, idiomatic expressions, and even recognize when multiple interpretations are possible, making it highly effective for applications like content generation, dialogue systems, and semantic analysis. For instance, Grok AI can engage in complex conversations, remembering previous interactions and adjusting responses based on the context. This contextual understanding allows Grok to have more natural, coherent exchanges with users, as it can make inferences about the conversation based on prior knowledge or statements. Additionally, Grok AI excels in machine translation, where it takes into account the context of the entire sentence, rather than translating word-by-word, which significantly improves translation quality and fluency.

5.3 Text Generation and Sentiment Analysis

One of the most exciting capabilities of Grok AI in the realm of NLP is its ability to generate human-like text. By using advanced language models, Grok AI can produce coherent and contextually relevant text, whether for writing articles, composing emails, or even generating creative content. This ability makes Grok AI useful for various industries, from content creation to customer service.

> Using Grok AI for Text Understanding

Grok AI's text understanding abilities extend beyond just reading and interpreting written content. It can summarize long articles, extract key pieces of information, and identify the sentiment conveyed in a piece of text. This is particularly useful for applications in business intelligence, where Grok AI can sift through vast amounts of text data, such as customer reviews or market reports, and extract actionable insights. Additionally, Grok AI can detect sentiment in text, helping organizations assess public opinion about their products or services. Sentiment analysis works by evaluating the tone of the text, categorizing it as positive, negative, or neutral. For example, Grok AI can be used to analyze customer feedback, social media posts, or product reviews, giving businesses a better understanding of consumer emotions and potential areas for improvement.

> Real-World NLP Use Cases

In customer service, Grok AI's text generation and sentiment analysis capabilities enable it to provide instant, context-aware responses to customer inquiries. Whether through a chatbot or an automated email system, Grok AI can analyze customer concerns and craft personalized, appropriate responses. This not only improves customer satisfaction but also reduces the burden on human agents, allowing them to focus on more complex issues. In content creation, Grok AI can help writers generate drafts or even complete articles, adjusting the tone and style based on the intended audience or the subject matter. This is particularly useful for businesses needing regular content for blogs, social media, or marketing materials, as it speeds up the content creation process while maintaining quality.

5.4 The Future of NLP with Grok AI

As AI continues to evolve, so too will the capabilities of Grok AI in NLP. The future of NLP holds significant promise, with advancements in areas such as multilingual understanding, better contextual reasoning, and deeper semantic analysis.

> Chatbots, Translation, and Customer Support

Chatbots powered by Grok AI are likely to become even more prevalent in customer support systems. These chatbots will evolve from simple question-answering systems to more advanced conversational agents capable of handling complex customer queries, understanding subtle cues in language, and offering personalized solutions. Grok AI's ability to understand context and maintain coherent conversations will play a central role in this transformation. In the field of translation, Grok AI will continue to improve the accuracy and naturalness of translations. As the system becomes more adept at understanding the cultural nuances and idiomatic expressions of different languages, it will make communication across linguistic boundaries even more seamless. This will be particularly useful for international business, where precise communication is critical.

> Challenges and Opportunities in Language Processing

While the future of NLP with Grok AI looks promising, there are still challenges that need to be addressed. One of the biggest hurdles is handling the diversity and complexity of human languages. There are thousands of languages, each with its own syntax, grammar, and cultural context. Building models that can accurately process and understand these languages will require significant advancements in training data and model architecture. Moreover, NLP models like Grok AI need to be continually updated to ensure they stay relevant and effective as language evolves. This is especially important when considering slang, new words, and rapidly changing trends in communication, which need to be integrated into models to keep up with real-time language shifts.

Despite these challenges, the opportunities for NLP with Grok AI are vast. Grok AI has the potential to revolutionize industries like healthcare, finance, education, and more by enhancing human-computer interactions. With continuous advancements, Grok AI's NLP capabilities will only become more refined, opening up new avenues for AI to improve daily life.

This chapter on Grok AI in Natural Language Processing provides an in-depth exploration of how the technology works, its current applications, and the significant impact it will have on the future of AI. With its advanced deep learning capabilities, Grok AI is poised to change the way we interact with machines, making communication smoother, more intuitive, and highly effective.

CHAPTER SIX

Grok AI and Computer Vision

6.1 Introduction to Computer Vision

> What is Computer Vision and Why it Matters

Computer Vision is a field of artificial intelligence (AI) that enables machines to interpret and understand the visual world. It involves the use of algorithms and models to process and analyze images and videos in ways that mimic human vision. The core goal of computer vision is to enable machines to "see" and make sense of visual data, much like how humans can recognize objects, understand scenes, and interpret the environment around them. For years, the vision of machines that could interpret images and videos seemed like a distant possibility. However, with advancements in deep learning and neural networks, particularly in the last decade, computer vision has made tremendous strides. Today, it is one of the most rapidly advancing fields in AI, contributing to the development of systems that can recognize faces, detect objects, and even analyze human emotions through visual cues. The importance of computer vision lies in its ability to automate processes that were previously reliant on human observation. In industries such as healthcare, automotive, security, and entertainment, computer vision is transforming workflows, improving accuracy, and enabling new capabilities. From detecting anomalies in medical images to enabling autonomous vehicles to navigate roads safely, computer vision has become an integral part of modern technology.

> Use Cases Across Industries

Computer vision is being applied in a wide range of industries. Some notable applications include:

- Healthcare: In medical imaging, computer vision is used to analyze X-rays, CT scans, and MRIs to identify conditions such as tumors, fractures, and organ abnormalities. Machine learning algorithms trained on vast datasets of medical images can help doctors make more accurate diagnoses and detect diseases in their early stages.

- Automotive: In autonomous driving, computer vision helps self-driving cars navigate roads, detect pedestrians, recognize traffic signs, and avoid obstacles. It allows these vehicles to understand their surroundings and make real-time decisions for safe and efficient navigation.

- Retail: In the retail sector, computer vision is used for tasks such as inventory management, shelf scanning, and cashier-less checkout. Cameras combined with AI algorithms help monitor stock levels, detect misplaced items, and even identify customer behavior patterns.

- Surveillance and Security: Video surveillance systems rely on computer vision to monitor security footage for suspicious activity. AI models can automatically detect intruders, track movement, and alert security personnel in real-time.

- Entertainment and Media: In video editing, AI-based tools help automate the tagging and organization of content. Additionally, deep learning is used in visual effects, making it possible to create highly realistic simulations and animations.

With its ability to process large volumes of visual data, computer vision is enabling innovations that improve productivity, enhance safety, and provide new insights across various sectors.

6.2 Grok AI's Visual Perception Capabilities

> How Grok AI Analyzes and Interprets Visual Data

Grok AI's visual perception capabilities are built on deep learning algorithms, particularly convolutional neural networks (CNNs), which are highly effective for image and video analysis. CNNs are designed to automatically detect and learn patterns from raw visual data, such as edges, textures, and shapes, which are essential for understanding complex visual scenes. When Grok AI processes visual data, the system first breaks down images into smaller parts or features, each representing a distinct element of the image, such as lines, colors, or patterns. These features are then analyzed and combined at higher levels to understand the content of the image. By learning from vast amounts of labeled data, Grok AI can recognize a wide range of visual objects and contexts. For instance, when tasked with identifying an object in an image, Grok AI uses its trained CNN to locate and classify features such as edges, corners, and textures, and then combines them to form a holistic understanding of the object. The AI does not rely on predefined rules or manual programming, but rather learns to identify objects autonomously by analyzing large datasets during its training phase.

Moreover, Grok AI's visual perception system continuously improves as it processes more data. This ability to learn and adapt means that the system can handle a wide range of visual tasks, from recognizing specific objects in highly variable conditions to interpreting dynamic scenes in real-time.

Understanding Images, Videos, and Real-World Environments

Grok AI is capable of interpreting both static images and dynamic video data. In image analysis, the system identifies and classifies objects within a single frame. However, when dealing with video, Grok AI must not only identify objects across multiple frames but also understand the relationships and interactions between objects over time.

This ability to interpret videos involves not only object detection but also motion tracking, event recognition, and context understanding. For example, in a surveillance setting, Grok AI can track a moving object, recognize its behavior (such as whether it is a pedestrian crossing the road or a car making a turn), and predict its future trajectory. This capability allows the system to understand real-world environments in a more dynamic and continuous manner, which is crucial for applications like autonomous driving and real-time monitoring. Grok AI's integration of visual perception and environmental understanding makes it well-suited for tasks that require a deep comprehension of the visual world, such as navigation, object manipulation, and safety-critical applications.

6.3 Applications of Grok AI in Vision Tasks

> Object Recognition, Face Detection, and More

One of the most common applications of Grok AI's visual perception capabilities is object recognition. Grok AI can accurately identify objects in images and videos by matching them against learned models. This includes both common objects, such as cars and furniture, as well as more specialized items, such as medical equipment or machinery parts. In the retail industry, for example, Grok AI is used to automate inventory management by scanning shelves and identifying missing or misplaced items. Similarly, in the healthcare sector, it can be used to analyze medical images for specific anomalies, such as identifying tumors in X-ray scans or detecting fractures in bone images. Face detection is another important application of Grok AI. By analyzing facial features, Grok AI can identify individuals or detect specific facial expressions. This capability is widely used in security systems for facial recognition, where Grok AI can scan a crowd to identify known individuals, or in marketing to track consumer behavior by analyzing emotions in real-time. Beyond these tasks, Grok AI can also perform complex tasks like action recognition in video sequences (e.g., identifying specific actions such as running, jumping, or waving) and even analyzing the interactions between multiple objects and people in a scene.

> Real-World Use Cases in Healthcare, Retail, and Surveillance

Healthcare: In medical imaging, Grok AI is applied to detect and diagnose diseases by analyzing radiographic images. For example, Grok AI can identify early signs of cancer in mammograms or assist in evaluating the severity of heart conditions in echocardiograms. The system's ability to provide accurate, fast, and consistent analysis helps doctors make more informed decisions, often leading to better patient outcomes.

- Retail: Grok AI's object recognition system has transformed retail operations by enabling cashier-less checkouts, automated inventory tracking, and even customer behavior analysis. Cameras equipped with Grok AI can track customers' movements, identify the items they pick up, and process transactions without requiring a human cashier.

- Surveillance: Grok AI is extensively used in surveillance systems for security purposes. In airports, public spaces, and private buildings, the system can analyze video feeds in real-time, detect suspicious behavior, and alert security personnel about potential threats. It can also track individuals across multiple cameras and recognize if they are engaged in unusual activities, such as loitering or running in restricted areas.

6.4 The Future of Computer Vision with Grok AI

> Enhancing Autonomous Systems

The future of computer vision is closely tied to the development of autonomous systems, and Grok AI is playing a pivotal role in this transition. Autonomous systems, particularly self-driving cars, rely heavily on computer vision to navigate safely and efficiently. Grok AI enhances autonomous systems by providing real-time analysis of the vehicle's surroundings. Through cameras, sensors, and LiDAR, Grok AI processes visual data to identify obstacles, pedestrians, road signs, and other vehicles. This information is then used to make driving decisions, such as steering, braking, and accelerating.

In addition to improving safety, Grok AI's computer vision capabilities enable vehicles to learn from new environments and adapt to changing conditions. For instance, Grok AI can recognize roadwork zones, new traffic patterns, or even recognize a vehicle's specific characteristics for parking and maneuvering in tight spaces.

> Bridging the Gap Between AI and Human Vision

The long-term goal of computer vision is to replicate human vision, which is highly complex and nuanced. While current AI systems, including Grok AI, have made significant strides in image and video analysis, there remains a gap in fully understanding context, interpreting abstract concepts, and recognizing subtle cues. However, as Grok AI continues to advance, it is expected that AI will get closer to human-like vision, not only recognizing objects but understanding the deeper context within visual data. This includes interpreting emotions from facial expressions, understanding the emotional tone of an environment, and even predicting human actions based on visual cues. As we move forward, the future of computer vision with Grok AI promises not only enhanced capabilities in autonomous systems but also a deeper integration of AI into our everyday lives. By bridging the gap between AI and human vision, Grok AI will redefine how machines interact with the world, bringing us closer to a future where AI can see, understand, and engage with the world in a truly human-like way.

CHAPTER SEVEN

Ethical Considerations and Challenges of Grok AI

7.1 The Ethics of AI

The rapid development of artificial intelligence (AI) has prompted significant discussions about the ethical implications of its use. As AI systems like Grok AI continue to advance, they bring new challenges regarding fairness, bias, transparency, and responsibility. These concerns need to be addressed, as AI systems increasingly influence daily life, business operations, and even personal decisions.

> **Bias, Fairness, and Transparency in AI Systems**

One of the most pressing ethical concerns in AI is bias. AI systems, including Grok AI, are trained using vast datasets that often reflect the existing biases in society. These biases can manifest in various ways, such as racial, gender, or socioeconomic biases. If not properly mitigated, these biases can lead to unfair outcomes, such as discriminatory hiring practices or biased predictive policing systems. Bias in AI is primarily a result of the data used to train these systems. If the data contains imbalances, such as underrepresentation of certain groups or historical patterns of discrimination, AI models will likely replicate those patterns. Grok AI, as an advanced system, is not immune to these challenges. The responsibility of ensuring fairness in AI lies with the developers and the institutions deploying these systems. It is essential to continuously audit and update AI models to detect and address potential biases. Fairness in AI is another significant ethical consideration. Fairness refers to the idea that AI systems should treat all individuals equally, without favoring one group over another. Grok AI's design and development aim to promote fairness by using diverse, representative datasets and employing fairness-enhancing algorithms. However, achieving perfect fairness is often difficult because different stakeholders might have conflicting views on what constitutes fairness in a given context.

Transparency is equally crucial in AI ethics. AI systems, including Grok AI, are often perceived as "black boxes," meaning that their decision-making processes are not always clear to users. Without transparency, users cannot trust or understand the reasoning behind AI decisions. This lack of clarity can lead to misunderstandings or the misuse of AI technologies. Therefore, Grok AI's developers emphasize creating systems that provide clear and understandable explanations for the decisions made by the model. Transparent AI systems allow users to hold AI accountable for their actions and ensure that the outcomes align with ethical standards.

> Responsibility in AI Decision-Making

As AI systems like Grok AI become more autonomous, the issue of responsibility becomes increasingly important. When an AI system makes a decision, such as approving a loan, diagnosing a medical condition, or recommending a job candidate, it is essential to determine who is accountable for that decision. If Grok AI makes an incorrect recommendation, is it the responsibility of the AI developer, the organization using the AI, or the AI itself? Currently, responsibility for AI decision-making largely falls on the developers and organizations deploying these systems. This responsibility extends to ensuring that the

AI is trained and tested properly, that it is free from bias, and that it operates in line with ethical standards. As AI technology advances, there is ongoing debate about how to allocate responsibility, especially in the case of fully autonomous systems. Ensuring that the decision-making process of AI systems like Grok AI is ethical and just is crucial for maintaining public trust.

7.2 Privacy and Data Protection

In order for AI systems like Grok AI to function effectively, they require vast amounts of data. This data can include personal information, such as medical history, financial records, and online behavior. The use of such sensitive data raises significant privacy concerns. As AI becomes more pervasive, ensuring that users' privacy is protected has never been more important.

> How Grok AI Handles Sensitive Data

Grok AI is designed with privacy and data protection at the forefront of its development. It uses state-of-the-art encryption techniques to ensure that sensitive data is stored and processed securely. By anonymizing and de-identifying data wherever possible, Grok AI minimizes the risks associated with handling personally identifiable information (PII). This ensures that users' personal information remains confidential and is not misused.

Additionally, Grok AI complies with global data protection regulations such as the General Data Protection Regulation (GDPR) in Europe and the California Consumer Privacy Act (CCPA) in the United States. These regulations set strict guidelines on how personal data can be collected, stored, and used. By adhering to these laws, Grok

AI ensures that users have control over their data and that their privacy is respected throughout their interactions with the system.

> Balancing Innovation and User Privacy

While it is essential for AI systems to protect user privacy, it is equally important to foster innovation. Grok AI must strike a balance between using large datasets to improve its functionality and ensuring that users' personal information is not compromised. This balance is critical because AI systems require vast amounts of data to be effective, yet over-collection of personal data could lead to privacy violations. Grok AI addresses this challenge by employing privacy-preserving techniques such as federated learning, which allows AI models to be trained on decentralized data without compromising user privacy. This approach enables Grok AI to learn from data while keeping sensitive information on users' devices, reducing the risk of data breaches or misuse. By prioritizing both privacy and innovation, Grok AI can continue to advance without compromising user trust.

7.3 The Impact of Grok AI on Jobs and Employment

The introduction of advanced AI systems like Grok AI has sparked debates about their potential impact on jobs and employment. Some argue that AI could displace millions of workers, while others believe that it will create new job opportunities. Understanding the true impact of Grok AI on the workforce requires a careful analysis of how AI will transform various industries.

> Job Displacement vs. Job Creation

One of the primary concerns surrounding AI is the potential for job displacement. As AI systems become more capable, they are increasingly able to perform tasks traditionally carried out by humans. For example, Grok AI can automate tasks in industries like customer service, data analysis, and even healthcare, potentially leading to job losses in these sectors. However, this is not necessarily a one-sided issue.

While AI may lead to job displacement in certain industries, it can also create new job opportunities. Grok AI's development and deployment require a skilled workforce, including AI researchers, data scientists, and engineers. Moreover, as AI continues to revolutionize industries, it will lead to the creation of entirely new sectors and job roles. For example, as AI becomes more integrated into healthcare, new opportunities may arise for individuals who can manage and interpret AI-driven diagnostics.

> How Grok AI Will Shape the Workforce of Tomorrow

In the future, Grok AI is expected to reshape the workforce by augmenting human capabilities rather than replacing them entirely. Rather than eliminating jobs, Grok AI will likely lead to the evolution of work. Many jobs will shift toward more creative, strategic, and human-centered roles, as AI handles routine and repetitive tasks. For example, in fields like marketing and customer support, Grok AI could automate mundane tasks such as data entry, allowing employees to focus on higher-value activities like customer relationship building and strategic planning. Similarly, in industries like healthcare, Grok AI could assist medical professionals by providing advanced diagnostic tools, but human judgment and empathy would remain essential in patient care.

7.4 Addressing AI Safety and Security Risks

As with any technology, AI systems come with potential safety and security risks. These risks range from the possibility of AI being used maliciously to vulnerabilities that could allow attackers to manipulate or compromise AI systems. Addressing these risks is essential to ensure that AI technologies like Grok AI remain safe and beneficial for users.

> Preventing Malicious Use of AI

One of the major concerns regarding AI systems like Grok AI is their potential for malicious use. Cybercriminals could exploit AI to conduct cyberattacks, such as automating phishing schemes or launching advanced malware attacks. Moreover, malicious actors could use AI to manipulate public opinion through fake news or social media bots. To address these concerns, developers must implement robust security measures to prevent AI systems from being hijacked for nefarious purposes.

Grok AI employs advanced security protocols to prevent unauthorized access to its systems. This includes secure authentication methods, real-time monitoring of AI activities, and the use of blockchain technology to verify the integrity of AI decisions. By ensuring that Grok AI is resistant to malicious use, developers can help protect users and organizations from potential harm.

> **Ensuring Grok AI is Safe for All Users**

AI systems like Grok AI must also be designed with safety in mind. As AI becomes more autonomous, the risks associated with incorrect or harmful decision-making increase. To ensure the safety of Grok AI, developers use a variety of testing and validation techniques to assess the AI's behavior under different scenarios. This includes stress testing, adversarial testing, and ensuring that the AI's decisions align with ethical and safety standards.

Furthermore, Grok AI's developers prioritize user safety by incorporating fail-safes and safeguards into the system. In the event that the AI encounters an issue or makes an unexpected decision, these safeguards can prevent the system from taking harmful actions. This proactive approach to AI safety helps ensure that

Grok AI can be used safely in a wide range of applications, from healthcare to finance.

In an increasingly AI-driven world, addressing these ethical, privacy, job, and safety concerns is vital. By doing so, Grok AI can contribute to the advancement of technology while ensuring that it aligns with societal values and principles.

CHAPTER 8

The Future of Grok AI and Artificial Intelligence

8.1 Predicting the Next Phase of AI Development

As we look toward the future of artificial intelligence, it is clear that the rapid advancements in AI, particularly in deep learning and neural networks, are leading us to a new era of technological possibilities. Grok AI, with its unique approach and powerful capabilities, is at the forefront of this progression. The following trends are expected to shape the next phase of AI development, with Grok AI playing a significant role in these shifts.

> **Trends to Watch in Grok AI and Deep Learning**

One of the most prominent trends in AI is the continued advancement of deep learning models, which Grok AI uses to process vast amounts of data and learn from it. Deep learning, characterized by its use of artificial neural networks, has already shown impressive capabilities in areas such as image recognition, natural language processing, and autonomous systems. However, we are still in the early stages of its potential.

In the coming years, we can expect deep learning algorithms to become more efficient and capable of handling even more complex tasks. Grok AI is likely to incorporate more advanced models, such as transformers, that have already revolutionized NLP tasks. These models are known for their ability to manage large amounts of sequential data, which is essential for processing human language, images, and even video. The integration of these more powerful architectures will lead to breakthroughs in machine understanding and generate even more sophisticated AI systems.

Another significant trend is the focus on interpretability and transparency in AI models. While Grok AI already excels in deep learning tasks, it is important to make these models more transparent. AI decision-making can sometimes be seen as a "black box"—where the model's reasoning is not easily understood. To address this, future versions of Grok AI may incorporate explainable AI (XAI) techniques that allow humans to better interpret how decisions are made. This trend is particularly important as AI continues to be integrated into critical sectors such as healthcare, finance, and transportation.

Finally, the development of "generalized AI" or Artificial General Intelligence (AGI) is an area that Grok AI may one day venture into. While today's AI models, including

Grok AI, are exceptional at performing specific tasks, AGI would represent an AI system capable of understanding and performing a broad range of tasks with human-like reasoning. Researchers are still far from creating AGI, but it remains a long-term goal for AI developers, including the team behind Grok AI. As progress is made in this area, AI could transition from specialized tools to more versatile, adaptable systems.

> The Role of AI in Industry 4.0

Industry 4.0, also known as the fourth industrial revolution, marks the shift from traditional manufacturing methods to smarter, more interconnected systems. The integration of AI, machine learning, and automation technologies is central to this transformation. Grok AI is poised to play a pivotal role in driving these changes. In manufacturing, Grok AI can optimize production lines by predicting equipment failures before they happen and improving efficiency through real-time data analysis. By leveraging IoT devices and AI algorithms, factories can become more responsive to demand and reduce waste, leading to more sustainable practices.

In supply chains, Grok AI can streamline operations by predicting trends, identifying inefficiencies, and enabling smarter inventory management. This level of automation and intelligence is essential for businesses to remain competitive in an increasingly complex global economy.

Beyond manufacturing, AI's impact on industries such as healthcare, finance, and retail will also accelerate. Grok AI's ability to analyze vast amounts of data in real-time will revolutionize diagnostics, fraud detection, customer service, and personalized marketing. The integration of AI into every facet of business and industry is shaping up to be one of the most transformative aspects of the next phase of technological development.

8.2 Grok AI's Potential Impact on Society

Artificial intelligence has already begun to reshape our society, and as Grok AI continues to evolve, its influence will expand into virtually every domain of life. The following areas are where we will see some of the most profound changes brought about by AI technologies like Grok.

> Healthcare, Education, and the Economy

AI's potential to improve healthcare is immense. Grok AI, with its deep learning capabilities, is already being used to analyze medical images, identify patterns in patient data, and predict potential health risks. As Grok AI becomes more advanced, it could take on a more proactive role in healthcare, helping to not only diagnose conditions but also recommend personalized treatment plans based on an individual's unique genetic makeup, lifestyle, and environmental factors. This would result in more precise and efficient medical care, potentially saving lives and reducing healthcare costs. In education, AI has the potential to provide personalized learning experiences tailored to the needs of each student. Grok AI's ability to analyze individual learning styles and progress could lead to highly customized curricula that help students achieve their full potential. AI-driven educational tools could support teachers by automating administrative tasks, allowing them to focus more on student engagement and teaching.

The economic impact of Grok AI is equally profound. AI technologies have the potential to drive significant productivity gains, particularly in industries such as manufacturing, logistics, and services. As Grok AI optimizes processes, businesses will be able to offer higher-quality products and services at lower costs. Additionally, Grok AI could create new industries and job opportunities, particularly in the tech sector, as demand for AI expertise grows. However, these advancements will also require careful management of the workforce transition to ensure that displaced workers are given the support and training they need to adapt to new roles.

> Social Good and Global Benefits of AI

Grok AI's potential for social good is vast. AI can be harnessed to address some of the world's most pressing challenges, including climate change, poverty, and global health crises. For instance, Grok AI can optimize energy consumption by predicting demand and improving efficiency in power grids, helping to reduce carbon emissions. In agriculture, AI-powered systems could help farmers optimize crop yields and reduce waste, making food production more sustainable. In developing regions, Grok AI could improve access to education, healthcare, and financial services by providing affordable, scalable solutions. AI-based systems could help bridge the gap in access to quality education and healthcare, especially in rural or underserved communities. AI-driven financial technologies could provide people with access to banking services, credit, and insurance, promoting economic inclusion.

Furthermore, Grok AI can assist in disaster response and humanitarian efforts. By analyzing data from satellites, drones, and other sources, Grok AI could help predict natural disasters and optimize relief efforts, ensuring that resources are allocated efficiently to those in need.

8.3 The Road Ahead for Grok AI

As we look to the future, the road ahead for Grok AI is filled with potential breakthroughs and research directions that could dramatically change how AI interacts with the world.

> Research Directions and Breakthroughs on the Horizon

The most immediate research direction for Grok AI is in the area of reinforcement learning. This branch of machine learning allows AI systems to learn from interactions with their environment, adapting their behavior based on rewards or penalties. Grok AI could evolve to incorporate more sophisticated reinforcement learning models, enabling it to solve problems in dynamic, real-time environments. This could revolutionize industries such as robotics, autonomous vehicles, and personalized marketing. Another area of focus is unsupervised learning, where AI systems learn from data without explicit labels. Grok AI could use this technique to uncover hidden patterns and insights from unstructured data, such as social media posts, news articles, and user behavior. This ability to analyze unstructured data is crucial as more and more information is generated in these formats.

AI safety and ethics will also remain a critical area of research. As Grok AI becomes more capable, ensuring that it operates transparently, fairly, and securely will be essential. Researchers will continue to work on creating AI systems that can explain their decisions, prevent biases, and protect user privacy.

> How Grok AI Can Change the World

Grok AI's potential to change the world lies in its ability to tackle complex, real-world problems that require deep understanding and analysis. Whether it's addressing healthcare challenges, improving education, or optimizing industrial processes, Grok AI has the power to enhance the efficiency and quality of life for people around the globe.

8.4 Embracing AI's Future with Grok

The future of AI is bright, and Grok AI is well-positioned to lead the charge in shaping that future. As AI continues to evolve, it will play an increasingly central role in driving innovation across industries, improving quality of life, and solving global challenges.

> The Journey to a Smarter, More Efficient World

As we move forward, embracing AI technologies like Grok AI will help us unlock new levels of productivity, sustainability, and human potential. AI has the power to enhance human capabilities, improve decision-making, and drive solutions to some of the most significant challenges of our time.

How You Can Get Involved in the AI Revolution

For those interested in joining the AI revolution, there are numerous opportunities. Whether you are a student looking to learn more about machine learning and deep learning, a professional seeking to integrate AI into your business, or someone passionate about ethics and AI safety, there is a growing community of individuals and organizations dedicated to advancing AI technologies. Grok AI is just one example of the transformative power of AI, and as the field continues to grow, it will offer even more ways to get involved and contribute to shaping a smarter, more efficient world.

CONCLUSION

As we stand on the cusp of a new era driven by artificial intelligence, Grok AI represents not just a leap in technology but a transformation in the way we understand and interact with the world around us. Its capabilities are far-reaching, touching every sector from healthcare to education, manufacturing to entertainment. As we've explored throughout this book, the potential of Grok AI to enhance human life is vast, with profound implications for industries, society, and global progress. From its innovative use of deep learning and neural networks to its role in the future of Industry 4.0, Grok AI is shaping the future of AI itself. As we embrace these advancements, we also face critical challenges in ensuring ethical development, security, and inclusivity. Yet, with careful thought, collaboration, and responsibility, the future of AI—embodied by Grok AI— holds unprecedented promise.

The road ahead is filled with endless possibilities. With each breakthrough, Grok AI can drive new applications, smarter systems, and more sustainable solutions, all while continuing to evolve and adapt to our ever-changing needs. The impact of AI on society will only grow, offering us opportunities to create a smarter, more efficient, and equitable world.

As we conclude this exploration of Grok AI and its transformative capabilities, we encourage you to continue to follow and engage with the evolving AI landscape. Your understanding, participation, and insights are crucial in shaping this revolution. If you've found this book insightful and engaging, please consider leaving a review. Your feedback helps us continue to share and refine the knowledge that drives our shared future.